Our Hearts Strangely Warmed:
A Practical Theology for Worship in the Wesleyan Tradition

A Call to Reclaim Who We Are as a Wesleyan/Methodist People

By D. Jonathan Watts

Library of Congress
LOC 2014930941
ISBN 978-155605-456-3

EBook Version 978-155065-457-0

Wyndham Hall Press
5050 Kerr Rd.
Lima, OH 45806

Contents

Our Hearts Strangely Warmed:

A Practical Theology for Worship in the Wesleyan Tradition

By Jonathan Watts

Dedication

I would like to dedicate this work to memory of Rev.
Charles H. Howard, Elder of the North Alabama
Conference of the United Methodist Church.
Rev. Howard gently guided me down the paths of
Methodism and instilled within me the desire for good
preaching and Godly worship.

I cherish the memories of his instruction, the sound of his
voice, and honor of him baptizing my oldest child.

Prologue

In 2010, I had published a book titled *The Battle Lines of Worship: Finding a Place of Truce and Trust.* The work was a response to a statement made in an adult Sunday School Class where I attend church. The lesson was on "right worship," and I began by simply stating John Wesley's approach to worship – we all do not have to do it the same way. This created a firestorm of discussion, and afterward I decided to write something that would help defuse the tension. I begin the book in Genesis when no form of formal worship existed. From there the book journeys through the Judeo/Christian heritage and ends with the struggle many churches have between their two forms of worship experience, often termed contemporary and traditional.

After conducting several seminars on the book, I found many attributes of the "contemporary" style of worship making its way into the "traditional" worship service. Screens now occupy a conspicuous place in the sanctuary and projectors are suspended from the rafters. Hymnals are no longer needed as the words are projected on the screen. The traditional service has been manipulated to accommodate the pastor's style used in the contemporary service. This blending and imprinting into the traditional worship service creates a tension. I have experienced that tension first hand. I pastored churches where I was placed in one environment at 8:30 a.m. (contemporary/post-modern) and a completely different setting at 11:00 a.m. (traditional/classical).

In the juggling of styles and traditions I noticed elements being left by the wayside that, in the past, were considered benchmarks of the Methodist service. I also was aware of the distancing of many churches from their denominational affiliations. I have often said, and it will be said again, God had a hand in the denominational expansion of the church. In God's wisdom there is a church that fits every personality, spiritual desire, and peer make-up. The United Methodist Church is the church I choose because I strongly believe in its theology, polity, and mission. In the ebb and flow of time I became aware that "my" church was becoming something other than "Wesleyan/Methodist."

I applied for a fellowship through The Graduate Theological Foundation, packed my bags, and headed back to Oxford, England, the birthplace of Methodism, to do research and find time to think. I spent hours in the basement of the Bodleian Library's Radcliffe Camera theological section and sorting through texts written in the 1700s. I walked the cobblestone paths the Wesleys may have traveled. Eventually, I made my way back to London, hopped the Tube to Liverpool, and walked north to Wesley Chapel and John Wesley home. I did everything I could to immerse myself in the spirit of Wesley's vision for Methodism.

Even though this swork can stand, alone it is intended to be a supplement to *The Battle Lines of Worship* book. It specifically moves from the general to the specific, the church at large to my church – the United Methodist Church.

Before I begin let me offer special thanks to two very important individuals. I want to extend a big thank you to Dr. Cynthia Denham, Director of the Humanities Division at Snead State Community College. She freely offers her time and talents in language and grammar in order to put my ramblings into proper English.

Also I say thank you to my wife Karen. When I would get that distant gleam in my eye and mention the possibility of working on a "book" she would first give me "the look!" Yet through it all, she has been more than patient with this wanderer, ponderer, and scribbler.

I also need to acknowledge a major portion of the research for this work was conducted at the Bodleian Library, Oxford University, England, under the direction of Rev. Dr. Robin Gibbons, Director of Studies in Theology and Religious Studies, Oxford University and Dean of Studies in Oxford, Graduate Theological Foundation in fulfillment of the designation of Oxford Foundation Fellow.

I offer this work with a prayer asking that you read this work with an open mind and do not find it critical but educational.

A CALL TO ACTION

I had the honor of sitting under the tutelage of the late Bishop William R. Cannon. Bishop Cannon taught classes in Early Methodist History and The Life and Theology of John Wesley at Candler School of Theology, Emory University. Dressed as a proper clergyman, this man of tall stature would stride into the classroom with a folder of notes and a class roll. He was described as being classically orthodox and Wesleyan. After Bishop Cannon called roll, he would glance down at the list and solicit the service of a student; "Mr. Watts, would you open the class with prayer?" The strong voice echoed the lecture hall with a deep accent rooted in the Southern heritage.

After glancing down to a marker where he had ended the prior lecture, he looked up and began his artistry of words. He used only his notes as a tool to remind him where the last session concluded. His gift was imagery. Bishop Cannon carried us into a different culture describing the founder's voices and dress and thoughts. When the course was complete not only did we know the history, but we could also describe the characters.

Rarely did he stray from the path of process and history, but I do remember one day with distinction. Deep into a discussion on the formation of the Methodist Episcopal Church, he wandered into the realm of titles and names. The Bishop's commanding voice thundered his displeasure at the *Merging Conference* labeling our church as "United." It was not so much the word as it was the connotation of that word. "'United' means we will try to be all things to all people and eventually we will be nothing to no one," he declared.

Much to my dismay, his words became prophetic. We are fast approaching at *that* place. We have bent over backwards to please and appease so as to keep peace and to entice those on the outside to come inside. This is played out so plainly on Sunday morning. Some have given up an order of worship so as to not make anyone uncomfortable. Some have cast aside the anchor points of the faith, the prayers and creeds, to make room for more music and longer sermons. Some have even changed the words that the early fathers and mothers so boldly declared for fear of someone misinterpreting its meaning. In the creed, the "holy catholic church" has been replaced with the word "universal" because the other word seemed so - well - Catholic. And to top it all, some now hide our denominational name (or at least put it in small print) so we appear to be a "community church" and not a United Methodist Church.

Over the past few years we have seen an abandoning of church labels. People no longer attend a church because of its title but because they find a connection to those persons who gather in that place. That concept becomes a two-edged sword with one side being theology and the other side being worship. We have failed as a church to educate those coming into our community on United Methodist theology and polity. This point of neglect often leads to disruption. One recurring example is when a pastor is "sent" to another parish. Persons complain because the congregation did not get to vote on the pastor. No, they do not - because that is not the way it is done in the United Methodist Church. Another example is why we do not baptize a person more than once. These are topics that should be discussed <u>before</u> individuals join the church not after they are a part of the community.

The other side of the sword, the worship side, again is in turmoil because of our rush to "put people to work." Those with an artful side we often assign to the worship committee. Without a background in liturgy and rubric, the persons in charge of worship begin to dismantle tradition and purpose. They have no idea why we wear green, or the Gospel Lesson of the day in Year A, or why it is important to say an affirmation and pray the Lord's Prayer.

More than once I have defended an act or action in worship against those who would discard it because they do not understand the significance or history behind the act. And, after I have taken time to explain the creed, prayer, or pattern, persons respond in amazement, "Oh! Now I understand!" and find a deeper worship experience because they "know" why we do what we do in worship.

In an earlier work *The Battle Lines of Worship: Finding a Place of Truce and Trust* (Wyndham Hall Press, 2010), I address the tensions between those who worship in the classical/traditional style and those who worship in the contemporary/post-modern style. This is a historical process beginning in Genesis and ending in the church today. It is an effort at making sense of how worship developed and realizing that indeed no one has a claim to "right" worship. Now I turn my focus on my own family in hope that we who call ourselves by the name Methodist can come to a better understanding of why we, as Wesleyan in theology, do what we do in worship.

Before we disappear in the mire of pluralism and post-modernism, we as a people called Methodist need to stand up and reclaim whose we are, who we are, and what we believe. It is time to reclaim the elements that so faithfully linked us, not only with other Methodist congregations but also back to the very roots of the catholic church - the church of Jesus Christ. We do not need to be "all things to all people." We need to be Methodist who should claim the heritage of helping the poor and needy, of offering up passionate prayers and songs, and of worship which includes liturgy and pattern. After all, it was because of John and Charles Wesley's methodical way of personal devotion and accountability they were given the name "Methodist." My concern is that in a world full of disposable goods we all too often think there are elements of our faith and worship we can simply throw away because some think they are old and worn.

There were two personal experiences that gave impetus to this work. The first occurred in 2001, while studying at Oxford University. One Sunday morning I attended the Eucharistic Service that was conducted in the Military Chapel of Christ Church Cathedral (a small space just off of the main nave). There were only a few people who had gathered, and I moved to sit next to an elderly man on the left side of the chapel. I still can hear the creaking sound of that old straight-back, wicker-bottom chair echoing across the stone surfaces as I sat down. As the service began, I found myself fumbling and flipping through the pages of the *1662 Prayer Book*. The elderly gentleman, sensing my misdirection, would graciously reach over and turn my *Prayer Book* to the correct page. He had no need to use his book – he had memorized the entire liturgy. During this early morning service the priest did not offer up a homily or sermon. As I exited the space, two very distinct impressions were made. First, as worshipers left the chapel they did so by walking under a passageway inscribed with the words: Fear God, Love the Brotherhood, Honor the King. The second impression was the realization that no word was spoken in the service which was not printed in the text of the *1662 Prayer Book*.

The second experience came in May, 2011, when I returned to Oxford to do research in fulfillment of my receiving an Oxford Foundation Fellowship from the Graduate Theological Foundation. I spent hours in the lower level of the Radcliffe Camera, an extension of the Bodleian Library, plowing through the rich fields of academia. When I returned to London, I made my way to Wesley's home and Chapel. I was greeted early that morning by a most cheerful elderly lady who gave me instructions on how to maneuver through the John Wesley museum. She also offered graciously to take my picture standing in Wesley's pulpit rescued from the Foundry, the first headquarters of Methodism.

I was slowly making my way through the exhibit

when she came to me whispering, "There is a large group of people due to arrive shortly for a tour. If you are ready, I can take you over to Mr. Wesley's home before they arrive."

I had a one-on-one tour of the home and chapel. Suddenly all those things that seemed so distant and mysterious about John Wesley became so personal and so real. The basement kitchen where he stored his spices. His study that faced the cemetery where his mother was buried. The bedroom made famous by the deathbed painting with 19 people gathered and the realization the painting greatly stretched the size of the room. I was amazed the home of this larger-than-life saint was comprised of such small rooms. Because of this visit, I experienced a shift from Wesley the legend and mystery to Wesley a real man filled with passion.

This is the first of two units that explore the topic of worship heritage. The first part is a brief historical journey through the development of the worship heritage of the people called Methodist. The second part will address specific elements and actions within the Methodist worship experience. I want to examine the Awhy@ we pray the prayer, say the creed, and sing the song. This does not apply only to those who attend classical/traditional worship. It is also a call to those in the contemporary/post-modern camp to insert back into their worship the elements which separate us from the rest of the world - elements of our Wesleyan heritage.

CHRISTIAN WORSHIP:FROM THE BEGINNING TO THE ENGLISH SCHISM

Worship before 300 AD was very simple. This was the case primarily because the worship space was often small – in homes (house churches) or in secret places. "Primitive" worship, as it is often referred to, consisted of the following: the gathering, a song (or songs), prayers, the pronouncing of a credo (this I believe), telling the stories of Jesus, the celebrating of the holy meal, and the sending forth of persons into the world.

The victory of Constantine over Maxentius for control of the western part of the Roman Empire was attributed to a mysterious sign given to Constantine the night before the battle. While praying for victory Constantine saw two Greek letters, chi and rho ($\chi\rho$) in a vision. Hearing a voice, "Under this sign you will conquer," he immediately instructed his army to paint the symbol on their armor. After his victory, Constantine embraced the notion that he was "emperor of the Christians." With the signing of the Edict of Milan by Emperor Constantine, who ruled the western parts of the empire, and Licinius, who ruled the eastern parts of the empire, Christianity not only came out of hiding but eventually became the religion of the empire.

The Church Exposed now needed larger places to worship. They utilized the Byzantine style of architecture, and churches were built all over the Roman Empire. Many churches were built in the cities of those considered to be saints with some actually built over the saint's grave. Later in history the idea was continued even in our tradition by naming churches "X" Memorial Church.

An internal struggle rose out of their exposure over theological differences. These churches, which before had operated in seclusion and isolation, now realized their ideas and concepts of the faith had taken different paths. Bickering and strife became public. This led to Emperor Constantine initiating the Council of Nicea in 325 AD that established the boundaries of the faith and embraced a common credo - The Nicene Creed.

The Church's influence grew in breadth and power. Churches became the anchor point for many communities. Priests became persons of influence and persuasion. Worship became ordered and precise.

At this point I open the curtain, as it were, midway in the story of church history. The church in England, at the beginning of the 16th century, was Roman Catholic. Cathedrals, basilicas, and churches were scattered across the landscape. One could imagine worshipers moving from their small houses and wandering over the green hills of England only to end their journey by entering the sanctuary amidst an atmosphere of ancient language and mysterious worship rubric. The Church followed orders of liturgy known as the York Missal or Sarum Missal. Windows detailing the life and teachings of Jesus, icons of the saints, and tapestries depicting holy moments adorned the sanctuary. The priests would vest themselves and the worship space in the colors of the liturgical season. Light from wax candles offered a warm glow. The smell of incense filled the air as the smoke rose symbolizing prayers rising up to Heaven.

The people nested themselves within the Sanctuary first standing the entire service and later instituting benches. This practice found its way into the church because of the great plagues and people, who were too weak to stand and fearing death, needed a place to sit. The priest began the liturgy of worship in a language understood only by the priests and God. *Deus qui corda fidelium Sancti Spiritus illustratione docuisti: da nobis in eodem Spiritu recta sapere, et de eius semper consolatione gaudere. Per Dominum nostrum Jesum Christum, Filium tuum, qui tecum vivit et regnat in unitate eiusdem Spiritus Sancti Deus. Per omnia saecula saeculorum. Amen. (O God, Who did instruct the hearts of the faithful by the light of the Holy Ghost: give to us, in the same Spirit, to know what is right, and ever rejoice in His consolation. Through Jesus Christ, Your Son, our Lord, Who with You lives and reigns in the unity of the same Holy Spirit, God. World without end. Amen.)* This prayer should be very familiar to persons who have experienced the Walk to Emmaus as a version is read and recited known as The Prayer to the Holy Spirit.

As described in *The Battle Lines of Worship*, the language often led to misunderstanding. The priest would have his back to the congregants as he issued the rite of the Eucharist in Latin. The foreign words echoed over the hard surfaces of the church. Unable to understand the words the mysterious phrases became the genesis for a magical term. As the priest spoke the holy words over the bread and wine they mysteriously became the body and blood of Jesus. A misunderstanding of the Latin phrase *hoc est corpus* (this is my body) turned into the magical command "hocus pocus."

The order of worship had become more complex and was conducted by professionals who knew how to "do worship the right way." They processed into the sanctuary with dignity. They solemnly said prayers. They mechanically followed the structure (liturgy) Sunday after Sunday after Sunday. For the common person, the Sabbath experience was more about being *in the presence of* rather than *being a part in* the act of worship.

THE CHURCH OF ENGLAND AND THE PRAYER BOOK

In 1509 King Henry VIII appeared on the stage. Henry had a problem - his wife. He wanted an annulment from the Pope so he could remarry. Cardinal Thomas Wolsey was chosen as the instrument to accomplish this goal. Upon his failure to secure a speedy annulment from Queen Catherine in 1534, King Henry VIII issued his Act of Supremacy declaring that the churches in England were both Catholic and Reformed. Most parishioners would not even notice the change when they attended worship the next Sunday. Henry, who was staunchly Catholic, never wanted to create a new church but rather to create an English Catholic church. For all practical purposes, he declared himself the Pope of the Anglican Church (my words not his). The worship service, the Mass, continued to be the norm and was to be conducted in Latin. Little was done as far as "order" was concerned.

With Wolsey's failure, Thomas Cranmer was brought on board to begin shaping this new church. The year before (1533) Cranmer was named Archbishop of Canterbury. After the separation with Rome, Cranmer orchestrated several bold and earthshaking initiatives including the availability of a Bible in English and clergy being allowed to marry. A major shift came in 1544 with the passing of the *Act of Six Articles*. Cranmer, by the King's authority, morphed the Mass from Latin (the language of the ancients) to English (the vulgar language of the locals). This was not the first time this language change had occurred. In Germany, just a few years prior, Martin Luther stood up against the Roman Catholic authorities, creating the "protestant" church – later labeled the Lutheran Church. Two things rose out of that schism. First, preaching took center stage rather than the eucharist (Lord's Supper or Communion). Second, the worship service was conducted in the vernacular - German. Now those who congregated for worship in England heard the liturgy in their own language.

In 1547, Henry died and was succeeded by Edward VI who was only ten years old. Cranmer took full advantage of the opportunity to completely reform the church. The "Ordinance for Receiving Sacraments" allowed the common persons to receive both sacraments (bread and wine). In earlier times the common person balked at taking the elements of Communion out of a concern that if these elements actually did change into the body and blood of Christ they were partaking in cannibalism. The Church's response was to reserve the "blood of Christ" for the priest and the common person could partake in the bread (the body). Cranmer argued that the concept of the elements literally changing into the body and blood of Christ (transubstantiation) was not theologically correct since Christ, in His fullness, sat at the right hand of the Father. Instead, it was Christ's spirit that became present within the bread and wine and among the believers. Many credit Martin Luther with the consubstantiation concept, but in England it preceded Anglicanism through the Lollardy Movement associated with John Wycliffe and embraced by Anglican theology.

By 1549 Cranmer published the first edition of *The Book of Common Prayer*. The title was chosen because this was a book to be used by both clergy and laity. The liturgy had been completely translated to English in an attempt to "protestantize" the church. In 1552, the second edition was issued moving the Anglican Church more in the direction of protestant theology. One person said Cranmer attempted to keep the worship service God-centered and Bible-based.

One other historical note: to those on the outside of the Anglican Church, the shift from Roman Catholicism to Church of England was smooth and worry free. Nothing could be further from the truth. Cranmer, the champion of the Church of England, was burned at the stake for heresy at the hands of the Queen Mary (aka: Bloody Mary), who returned England to Catholicism. When I visit Oxford, England, I often go to the Saxon Tower constructed in 1040 AD. The tower is connected to St. Michael's Church where John Wesley preached the Michaelmas sermon in 1726 (the pulpit still stands in the church). The tower is located at the town center and at one point was used as a prison. As you climb the narrow steps of the tower you will find a glass case of artifacts of John Wesley. Proceeding up the stairs, you turn the corner and come face-to-face with a heavy blue door. This door once secured the entrance to a cell where Cranmer was held at the command of Bloody Mary. It created a sobering moment when I placed my hand on the door and imagined it opening for a faithful servant to move toward his execution.

After the death of Queen Mary and a tumultuous civil war, England again embraced Anglicanism. The work was revised and published as the *1662 Edition of The Book of Common Prayer*. This book continues to be the "authorized" version for worship in the Church of England. The Biblical texts for this version were the Great Bible of 1538 and the Authorized Version (King James) of 1611.

The *1662 Edition* seems to cover almost every situation a minister or congregant would encounter. There are directions and tables for the cycles of the church, reading of the day, worship liturgies, prayers, rites for baptism, weddings, confirmation, burial of the dead, ordaining of the clergy, and even services to be used while at sea.

The order of worship directed by the *1662 Prayer Book* was very precise and was separated by the service of Word (Morning and Evening Prayers) and the service of Communion (the Table). For the purpose of later reference, the service of Holy Communion follows a particular pattern with specific instructions (rubrics) for the words and movements of the priest:

1662 Book Of Common Prayer Service of Holy Communion

Introduction and Directions (fine linen cloth covering table)
The Lord's Prayer

A Collect for Purity (a collect is a short prayer)
The Decalogue (The Ten Commandments)

Collects for the King/Queen

Collect of the Day

The Epistle Lesson

The Gospel Lesson

The Nicene Creed

Parish Notices

The Sermon/Homily

Offertory Sentences and the Collection

Rubric for the Presentation of the Bread and Wine

Prayer for Christ's Church Militant

Warnings and Exhortations (not to come to the Table unprepared)

The Invitation

General Confession

Prayer of Absolution (Forgiveness)

Comfortable Words

Liturgy of Communion

The Sanctus

The Prayer of Humble Access

The Prayer of Consecration

Distribution of the Elements

The Lord's Prayer

The Prayer of Thanksgiving

FROM ENGLAND TO AMERICA

It seems to be a small step from 1662 to 1703. That was the year that John Wesley, fifteenth child of nineteen born to Samuel and Susanna Wesley, entered the world at Epworth, England. Samuel was an Anglican Priest in the parish at Epworth. John grew up to attend Oxford University and was ordained an Anglican Priest with his brother Charles at Christ Church College.

Volumes have been written on the life and influence of John Wesley. Stories are told of his life being saved from a burning house, the missionary trip to Georgia, the Holy Club or Bible Moth group which methodically disciplined their lives, and his "Heart Warming" experience on Aldersgate Street. I have taken seminary courses on his life, his theology, and the results of his labors.

As Wesley worked to reform England, the struggle of a birthing nation found itself victorious. Immediately the scores of Anglican Priests who served in America returned home. This left an enormous void of ordained clergy in the States. With a true servant's heart, Wesley (in an unprecedented move) ordained Thomas Coke for ministry in the Americas. Coke, along with Richard Whatcoat and Thomas Vasey, were sent to the new frontier with Wesley's words "Offer Them Christ." Thus began the journey of American Methodism.

Realizing these new ministers would be itinerant, Wesley designed his own order of worship. John Wesley, who remained an Anglican Priest, loved the *Book of Common Prayer* but realized the liturgy and rubric were too long and laborious.

In 1784 he created the *"Sunday Service of the Methodists in North America."* Using the basic pattern of the *Book of Common Prayer*, he adapted the service to be simpler and shorter.

Here is how the two services compare:

The Book of Common Prayer	Wesley's Sunday Service
Introduction and Directions	Introduction and Directions
The Lord's Prayer (Priest)	The Lord's Prayer (Minister)
A Collect for Purity (short prayer)	A Collect for Purity
The Decalogue (The Ten Commandments)	The Decalogue
Collects for the King/Queen	Collect for Supreme Rulers
Collect of the Day	Collect of the Day
The Epistle Lesson	Epistle Lesson
The Gospel Lesson	Gospel Lesson
The Nicene Creed	
Parish Notices	Parish Notices
The Sermon/Homily	Sermon
Offertory Sentences and the Collection	Offertory Sentences and the Collection
Rubric for the Presentation of the Bread and Wine	

Prayer for Christ's Church Militant	Prayer for Christ's Church Militant
Warnings and Exhortations	
The Invitation	The Invitation
General Confession	General Confession
Prayer of Absolution (Forgiveness)	Prayer for Pardon
Comfortable Words	Comfortable Words
Liturgy of Communion	Liturgy of Communion
The Sanctus	Sanctus
The Prayer of Humble Access	Prayer of Humble Access
The Prayer of Consecration	Prayer of Consecration
Distribution of the Elements (clergy first)	Distribution (clergy first)
The Lord's Prayer	Lord's Prayer
The Prayer of Thanksgiving	Prayer of Thanksgiving
The Gloria	The Gloria
	An Extempore Prayer
The Benediction.	The Benediction

Some notable points of change in Wesley's *Service* were that the word "minister" replaced the word "priest," extemporaneous prayers were allowed, and the Psalter became abbreviated. He also used the text of the *King James Version* for the entire service. Since the churches and chapels in the States were new congregations, Wesley replaced parts of the rubric that called for the congregation to sing with "the congregation will say." He removed all mention of clerical vestment. These mobile ministers would not have the luxury of large bags and the requirement to transport vestments would be cumbersome. He strongly advocated celebrating the Lord's Supper every Sunday. He also insisted on the "sign of the cross" to be continued during the prayer of consecration of the Eucharistic elements and during infant baptism.

At the Christmas Conference of 1784 the *Service* was adapted, but some elements were mysteriously changed or removed. The sign of the cross and also the inclusion of the line in the Apostle's Creed "he descended into Hell" disappeared.

After the death of John Wesley and the 1792 General Conference of the Church, the *Sunday Service* virtually disappeared.

THE MANIFEST DESTINY OF THE CHURCH

What followed was an expansive explosion of the church. Methodism (as well as other denominations) expanded their mission fields as the nation expanded its footprint on the continent. The Methodists seemed to embrace a "Manifest Destiny" position and wherever they found a Post Office or a major intersection of roads they were determined to build a church.

As a result, the clergy were stretched extremely thin. They stayed on the move following a circuit of small congregations. Most clergy did not have the luxury of pastoring a single church or even having an office. They traveled with everything they needed for work and worship - mostly a few clothes, a Bible, and maybe a hymnal. With this fluidness of the clergy movement, worship was kept very simple. They did not have the resources to conduct a formal liturgical service. Even though Wesley stressed the need for the Lord's Supper every Sabbath, the congregation experienced the gifts of bread and wine only on the days the minister was in town.

As time and expansion moved forward, industrialization became the catalyst for change. People began moving out of the "country" and into the city/urban areas where there was work. The church grew, and as a result pastors began to become more stable. Many churches had reached an economic level where they could retain the services of a single minister. This in turn brought about the rebirth of the liturgical worship experience. Ministers again began vesting in robes and stoles. The sanctuary regained the presence of liturgical color. There seemed to be a dual level of worship - one for the city folk and one for the country folk. The "country folk" continued in a very simple and humble style of worship and often used the "gospel" style of music. The "city folk" embrace the structured service. Because of the stable congregation, those worshiping in the traditional/classical form were able to enhance the worship service with musical instruments, choirs, anthems, and hymns.

The urban/suburban church again embraced the liturgy of worship in the developing hymnals and books of worship. Patterns for worship not only included the service of the Lord's Supper but also special services for almost any other special event in the life of the church or in the life of a church member. *The United Methodist Book of Worship* became, for all practical purposes, the Prayer Book of the Methodist people. The order for "A Service of Word and Table" can be found in that book as well as the *United Methodist Hymnal*.

Here is how the United Methodist Church service aligns itself with the *Book of Common Prayer* and Wesley's *Sunday Service*.

The Book of Common Prayer	Wesley's Sunday Service	Service of Word and Table
Introduction and Directions	Introduction and Directions	The Gathering and Greeting
The Lord's Prayer (Priest)	The Lord's Prayer (Minister)	Hymn of Praise
A Collect for Purity	A Collect for Purity	Opening Prayer
The Decalogue)	The Decalogue	Prayer for Illumination
Collects for the King/Queen	Collect for Supreme Rulers	The Old Testament Reading
Collect of the Day	Collect of the Day	The Psalm
The Epistle Lesson	Epistle Lesson	Reading from the Epistle
The Gospel Lesson	Gospel Lesson	Gospel Lesson
The Nicene Creed		
Parish Notices	Parish Notices	
The Sermon/Homily	Sermon	Sermon
Offertory Sentences and the Collection	Offertory Sentences and Collection	Response to the Word
Rubric for the Presentation of the Bread and Wine		
Prayer for Christ's Church Militant	Prayer for Christ's Church Militant	Concerns and Prayers
Warnings and Exhortations		
The Invitation	The Invitation	The Invitation
General Confession	General Confession	Confession and Pardon
Prayer of Absolution (Forgiveness)	Prayer for Pardon	Passing of the Peace
Comfortable Words	Comfortable Words	The Offering
Liturgy of Communion	Liturgy of Communion	The Great Thanksgiving
The Sanctus	Sanctus	
The Prayer of Humble Access	Prayer of Humble Access	

The Prayer of Consecration	Prayer of Consecration	The Lord's Prayer
Distribution of the Elements (clergy first)	Distribution (clergy first)	Breaking of the Bread
The Lord's Prayer	Lord's Prayer	Giving the Bread and Cup
The Prayer of Thanksgiving	Prayer of Thanksgiving	Prayer after Reception
The Gloria	The Gloria	
	An Extempore Prayer	Sending Forth Hymn
The Benediction.	The Benediction	Dismissal with Blessing

BEING ALL THINGS TO ALL PEOPLE.

The duality of city/country services seemed to stay intact until the 1960's when a bunch of west-coast hippies started the Jesus Movement. The buying into the culture's music and relaxed context developed into a style now identified as "contemporary" worship. This is not a historically correct term by definition since the very time in which anyone lives is contemporary. It is hard to conceive that once-upon-a-time Handel's *Messiah* was contemporary music.

The growth of the Contemporary Christian Community, mostly housed in store-front buildings, became a threat to the Mainstream Church. The young and young at heart began to migrate to this new worship experience. To meet the challenge of loss, the churches decided "if we can't beat them we will join them." So they rearranged fellowship halls, invested heavily in sound and media components, and stretched the clergy thin in the name of reaching out and holding on to those drifting away.

The result was a be-like-them mentality. They cast off their robes and stoles. They served coffee and food before, during, and after the service. They turned old rock-and-rollers into Praise Band members. The final blow was to throw away anything orthodox or "old church." The creeds and Lord's Prayer were left hanging in the traditional sanctuary. The songs were new and upbeat. And, more often than not, they left those gathered to reposition themselves as spectators of worship and not participants in worship.

The final blow came with two actions. First, not to offend or embarrass anyone, the church lost its sense of theology and identity. What made them Methodist or Presbyterian or Episcopal was gone. There was nothing left in the worship service lending itself to theological identification.

Second was the loss of exterior identity. Churches began renaming themselves so as not to not be identified with a particular denomination. The signs proclaimed "Christ Church," "Holy Mountain Church," "Top of the Hill Church" with nothing to identify their theology as Methodist, Baptist, or any other denomination.

What is to follow is an examination of the "why" we do what we do in worship and the life of the church which makes us who we are. I will explore the theology, doctrine, and purpose of the elements I consider the bedrock of who we are as Wesleyan/Methodist.

THE THINGS OFTEN LEFT BEHIND

I have often heard those who desire spiritual simplicity to declare they are "returning to the way the early church worshipped." They want the unencumbered gathering. They want a purer connection to the Holy. They seek the way it "was" in the "here and now." To accomplish this they discard anything from worship they sense as obstructive, cumbersome, or unimportant.

This is not a modern day story. It has been repeated over and over again since Martin Luther's Reformation. Luther attempted to reclaim some of the early church rite through the use of the vernacular language and preaching. The Amish attempted to regain the simplicity through uniform dress, beards, and sensitivity toward the Spirit. The Quakers cast out any form of "organized" worship. The Holiness and Pentecostals sought the experience through a special visitation of the Holy Spirit. Those who found themselves in the "new country" after the American Revolution discarded the "appearance" of things that cluttered the space. In the Protestant Reformation and Enlightenment much was left out of liturgy because it was too Catholic.

Two personal illustrations came rising up from the catacombs of my memories as I pondered the issues of worship. These, I think, describe where many churches are in worship today.

The first awakening came several years ago when I needed new soles for a pair of my favorite shoes. I walked into the repair shop and placed them on the counter. The shoe repair man took a shoe, and after closely examining the bottom, top and inside, informed me the shoes could not be repaired: "They make disposable shoes these days. Once you wear out the sole you just throw them away."

The second illustration was found in a commercial for an automobile company trying to explain the company's policy on commitment to quality. In the commercial the announcer said, "Don't like your nose – get a new one. Don't like your job – get a new one. Don't like your spouse – get a new one."

These illustrate the current mentality of so many who want to "go back" to the early church models by throwing away or discarding anything they do not like, do not understand, or do not have room for. But, to their surprise, it may be they are, as the old saying goes, "Throwing out the baby with the bath water." The early church did not simply sit around in chairs, singing songs, and daydreaming about heaven. The church had a formula for what was to happen when they gathered. The core of that formula is the anchor which holds the church today to a standard and remembrance of where we come from and to whom we belong. John Wesley himself recognized the burden of liturgical worship in a frontier setting and noted that those in the Americas were not bound by the *Sunday Service* but rather were simply to follow the Scriptures and the pattern of the Primitive Church. Frances Asbury defined that pattern as singing, prayer, readings from the Old Testament and New Testament, and preaching. Shortly after this order was issued, the inclusion of the Lord's Prayer, Apostle's Creed, and the Benediction also became added to the standard.

Coming to the forefront of the Christian movement over the past two decades were a few very successful "non-denominational" mega-churches crafted in a model of "contemporary style" or Post-Modern worship. Those in the denominational church decided they must complete and embrace this new pattern. Instead of taking the core traditions, theology, and culture of their local church and denomination then importing them into a new order of worship they simply threw out everything. The end result was a non-descript worship service defined as one with no order so the Holy Spirit would be free to lead and work. Often there are no Christian symbols displayed in the worship space; scriptures are offered to the people in little verses scattered throughout the message; and the creeds, prayers, colors, and special days are abandoned. All of this is done, in the words of a very prominent mega-church pastor, so that those gathering will not feel "uncomfortable" in the setting. My response to that statement: If these people are coming into a church environment then why should the symbols, music, and atmosphere of Christianity make them uncomfortable? Are we trying to be disciples of Christ through a clandestine approach - sneaking our faith and beliefs into a secular space in order to surprise the gathered?

That being said let me place a big emphasis on the purpose of this part of the work. It is not to cast blame, shadow, or doubt on anyone's integrity in worship. I do not propose, as often seems by those in the traditional camps, to cast us all back into the Middle Ages. It is not a call to discard all the praise bands, PowerPoints, and folding chairs from the church. What I simply ask is whichever style of worship you embrace there is, within the confines, the necessity and ability to claim who we are theologically, historically, and Biblically as Wesleyan / Methodist people.

Before I tread the treacherous waters of order and function let me establish a set of definitions – especially in regards to the title of this work: *A Practical Theology for Worship in the Wesleyan/Methodist Tradition.*

Practical: pertaining to the act or action of doing or using something which is effective in real life circumstances.

Theology: the act of focusing on or study of God.

Worship: the act and actions by which one connects to the Holy.

Wesleyan/Methodist: the basis of understanding and interpretation using the concepts of John Wesley and those who call themselves Methodist in the arenas of theology and doctrine.

Tradition: the conduit that connects the ancient with the contemporary – the roots of the family tree that define who we are as a church.

Wesley taught that we do not have to worship in the same way in every place. We seem to have taken that to heart. Even though we have patterns for worship in our United Methodist Book of Services and in the United Methodist Hymnal, each minister and congregation recreates the form into an order that meets the worship needs of the local congregation. For example, in the new order the offering is taken near the end of the service after the sermon/homily. Many pastors would poke fun at themselves saying they were losing money because this put extra pressure on their sermon. A bad sermon meant a low offering. And so they moved the offering to a more comfortable position – in the middle of the service.

If we set aside the titles of worship style, we find there are constants which are included in not only current worship traditions but also extend back to the early church itself. Those attributes are music, prayer, scripture, creed, sermon, communion, and baptism. These worship elements are the bones that make up the spine of the worship skeleton. If one of these attributes were to be cast aside the skeleton becomes weak.

Moving through these elements, I will address each of the worship attributes by defining each in three arenas – Worship Tradition, Wesleyan, and finally, Practical Theology.

MUSIC

Worship Tradition:

From the most ancient records of praise and worship in the Judeo/Christian tradition music has played a major role. In Genesis we read: *Jubal - was the ancestor of those who play stringed and wind instruments.* (Genesis 4:21 CEB) From its earliest history, human kind everywhere found music to be an extension of every part of our being. When we are happy, we sing. When we are troubled, we sing. And when we do not have the words to express our thoughts, we use the words of others who have been in our shoes.

By way of tradition, we sing because it is ingrained in spirits. It was an integral part of celebrating God's goodness in the earliest biblical stories. Miriam sang when they crossed the Red Sea. When it was time for Moses to die, God instructed him to write down a song. It was incorporated into the liturgy/order of worship in the Temple. It was included in the services held in the synagogues and even in the Upper Room. When Jesus took the disciples towards the garden, the non-canonical gospel The Acts of John tells how Jesus circled the disciples at the brook and together they sang a hymn. So, from a "tradition" standpoint, nothing has deeper roots than song and music.

When one enters into a traditional/classical worship service, the first sound heard is the chatter of a gathering community. Eventually the musicians (organ or piano) begin an instrumental prelude that becomes a signal to chat louder. This turns to reverent silence only when the liturgist or pastor addresses the congregants.

The contemporary/post-modern service begins with loud chatter and often loud music. This could be either instrumental or vocal. In a real sense, silence is an intentionally excluded attribute in the worship experience. Persons are encouraged to "act naturally" by getting up to get a cup of coffee or snack during the worship experience. This means the sound of mumbling, sliding chairs, and shuffling feet are a natural part of the worship experience.

In each of these traditions sound is defined in a different way. For one, sound is most holy when there is no sound at all. For the other, it is sound that drives one heavenward.

I have addressed the issue of music in the book *The Battle Lines of Worship* (Wyndham Hall Press, 2010), but let me simply restate some of my concepts. The difference between the traditional/classical church hymn and praise and worship music is its textual/contextual approach. Hymns, especially those of the John and Charles Wesley, Isaac Watts, and Martin Luther, were written to express and explain their theology. This is why, for these hymns, if you leave out a verse you skip a part of the theological train of thought or have an incomplete story. These hymns often take time to think through. One must ponder the depths of the text and evaluate the eternal consequences. Often the result is the worshipers create an identity with the tune and lyrics and will find these texts floating through their minds when the music seems appropriate for their current state of life. How many times have you gone through a traumatic event only to find yourself singing a song?

Later came the era of Gospel Hymns. Gospel Hymns often create stories of personal desire and hope – i.e.: a little log cabin in the corner of heaven, a mansion just over the hilltop, and singing in heavenly choirs. (Fun to sing but not theologically or biblically sound.) If you examine the context of many of these Gospel Songs, you will feel a "get me out of here" directive: "God, I will hang on until I get over there with You."

To me, the current trend of praise and worship music is part story and part affirmation. As a worshipers sing the story (often set in the context of the here-and-now), they reach a part I term the affirmation, which is often repeated over and over again. As with the Gospel Music, I find this music is designed to touch the heart and not so much the intellect. This music also becomes imbedded in the souls of the listener and is often repeated in the mind and from the lips in times of distress or praise.

Wesleyan:

Music is in the genetic make-up of the Wesleyan/Methodist tradition. Charles Wesley, depending on the source, is credited with writing between 6,500 and 9,000 hymns. John, although not as prolific, wrote many hymns himself. In a span of 53 years John and Charles Wesley produced 56 collections of hymns. One of my prized possessions is a Methodist Hymnal dated 1782. The book is only two inches wide, three inches tall, and about one and a half inches thick. The small print (maybe a 7-font) makes me wonder how persons in that era were able to read the words. There is not a musical note in the text – only "tune" titles which were imbedded in the fiber of the congregants. Methodist are often identified as a "singing people." Their "hymn cannon" (the specific songs a group of worshipers claim as their own) includes a wide variety of types and styles of music. We as Wesleyan/Methodist people express our theology, confess our sins, and seek the very face of God through our music.

Practical Theology for Today:

We often use music to define who we are or even what mood we are in. There are days when I need music to pick me up and push my spirit heavenward. There are other days when I am more reflective, and I need music which allows me to sink deep within my soul and gives me space to hear the voice of God. There is no "single" music that addresses all our spiritual attributes. We ourselves vacillate between the spheres of our emotion. There is the old saying that variety is the spice of life and in life it takes spices of all types. Each and every style of Christian music used within the church holds a special integrity of its own.

What I want to do is challenge those who construct the worship experience to pay close attention to the words, mood, and intention of their music. Selection of music is to be intentional and informed. Both current styles of worship (traditional/classical and contemporary/post-modern) base their worship on themes or texts. The one designing worship should ask, "Does this song, hymn, or anthem address the text/theme of the day?" Or simply put, be intentional.

PRAYER/LORD'S PRAYER

Worship Tradition:

At the core of our very existence is the desire, if not the pure spiritual drive, to connect with the Divine. Some scientists believe they have found proof the human brain is "hotwired" to seek God. The relationship between Creator and created was experienced in the Garden as Adam and Eve walked with God in the cool of the day. After the "fall of humanity" we have been relegated to the process of communicating with God through prayer – however that is defined and however it is expressed.

The Old Testament scriptures are filled with prayers. Prayers for protection. Prayers of joy and sorrow. Prayers asking God to rain down fire and destruction on another. In the Psalms one can find a prayer for almost every occasion. The prayer concept of the Jewish community was to go boldly and honestly to God. A person must approach God honestly because God already understands us better than we know ourselves. If we come to God in a posture other than total honesty and sincerity we deceive ourselves not God.

Jesus knew the powerful connecting force of prayer. Over and over again Jesus went to pray (carry on a conversation) with the Father. In the Sermon on the Mount Jesus warned those gathered about praying like the hypocrites: *"They love to pray standing in the synagogues and on the street corners so that people will see them."* (Matthew 6 5 CEB) I have heard some of those prayers – prayers that went on for what seemed like forever. I define those as the "Genesis to Revelation" prayers because the prayer covers the entire Bible, most of church history, with an added dash of guilt. There are times the pastor uses the Pastoral Prayer simply to get something "off their chest" they would be uncomfortable addressing in a face-to-face conversation.

As "adolescent" as it was, I remember in my youth having a pastor who loved long prayers. In fact, we (some youth in the church) would often "time" his prayers to see just how long his prayers lasted. Jesus warned against prayers filled with hollow words and repetitious phrases. Jesus set for us an example that illustrated both compactness and inclusiveness.

Jesus instructs his disciples by saying: *"Pray then in this way: Our Father in heaven, hallowed be your name. Your kingdom come. Your will be done, on earth as it is in heaven. Give us this day our daily bread. And forgive us our debts, as we also have forgiven our debtors. And do not bring us to the time of trial, but rescue us from the evil one."* (Matthew 6:9-13 NRSV)

Jesus understood the appropriateness of short, direct prayers. After all, if God indeed is omnipotent our prayers are more a reminder for us than a reminder for God. When Jesus finally arrived at his friend's grave, the family of Lazarus stood nearby as he wept and then offered a prayer: *And Jesus looked upward and said, "Father, I thank you for having heard me. I knew that you always hear me, but I have said this for the sake of the crowd standing here, so that they may believe that you sent me."* (John 11: 41b-42) The next image in the story is the man who had been dead for four days walking out of the tomb.

After Jesus ascended, we read in Acts 1: *Then they returned to Jerusalem from the Mount of Olives, which is near Jerusalem--a sabbath day's journey away. When they entered the city, they went to the upstairs room where they were staying. Peter, John, James, and Andrew; Philip and Thomas; Bartholomew and Matthew; James, Alphaeus's son; Simon the zealot; and Judas, James' son-- all were united in their **devotion to prayer**, along with some women, including Mary the mother of Jesus, and his brothers.* (Acts 1:12 – 14 CEB)

From this point forward every gathering of the People of God included prayers. Prayers invoke God's presence. Prayers lift up the concerns of the people. Prayers of thanksgiving are offered for all God has provided. A prayer sends the gathered into the world so they can "be" the church out in the world.

Prayer is an integral part of worship in whichever form that worship one prefers. I do not know of a church, traditional/classical or contemporary/post-modern in style, which does not open the worship experience with a prayer, offer a collective prayer (pastoral prayer) for and on behalf of the gathered people, and end with prayer to send them forth into the world. Some worship traditions include prayers after taking an offering or after spending time with the children.

Wesleyan:

John Wesley himself noted the following on the importance of prayer:

God's command to "pray without ceasing" is founded on the necessity we have of his grace to preserve the life of God in the soul, which can no more subsist one moment without it, than the body can without air.

Whether we think of; or speak to, God, whether we act or suffer for him, all is prayer, when we have no other object than his love, and the desire of pleasing him.

All that a Christian does, even in eating and sleeping, is prayer, when it is done in simplicity, according to the order of God, without either adding to or diminishing from it by his own choice.

Prayer continues in the desire of the heart, though the understanding be employed on outward things.

In souls filled with love, the desire to please God is a continual prayer.

As the furious hate which the devil bears us is termed the roaring of a lion, so our vehement love may be termed crying after God.

God only requires of his adult children, that their hearts be truly purified, and that they offer him continually the wishes and vows that naturally spring from perfect love. For these desires, being the genuine fruits of love, are the most perfect prayers that can spring from it.

(From *A Plain Account of Christian Perfection* – as taught by John Wesley)

I may also note, the most poignant prayer of the worship service is the Lord's Prayer. This prayer was included in the instructions to the Methodist people that Wesley himself sent across to a birthing church. It is indeed, for me, a sad state of the church when we as a Methodist people think we no longer need to pray the prayer Jesus taught us to pray because it is awkward or takes up too much time in the service.

Practical Theology for Today:

From a practical standpoint, prayer is simply talking to God. And especially in worship, every part/element of the gathering should be bathed in prayer.

I often hear words (which will be repeated again later) from those who say they do not like the Lord's Prayer because the language is strange. If I could be granted permission, let me shift a few words from the ancient to the common vernacular so we can hear the prayer most often said in our churches.

Our Father, who is in heaven, Holy is your Name.

Your Kingdom come. Your will be done in earth, as it is in heaven.

Give us this day our daily bread. And forgive us our trespasses, as we forgive those that trespass against us.

And lead us not into temptation, but deliver us from evil.

For yours is the kingdom, the power, and the glory, for ever and ever.

Amen.

When we pray this prayer at church many would like to contemporize the text but, when asked to pray, the congregation instinctively reverts to the implanted text of "thy" and "thine."

Is it too cumbersome to keep this prayer in our worship experience? Is there anything about this prayer that shifts the emphasis away from being either one who attends traditional/classical worship or contemporary /post-modern worship? The Lord's Prayer should be continued in every form of worship – not because it is a nice prayer but because it is the prayer Jesus himself taught us.

SCRIPTURE

Worship Tradition:

From the earliest traditions of worship, to read scripture and to tell the stories were the central core of worship. In the time between Adam and Moses, worship consisted of telling the stories of YHWH God and the promises made to humanity.

From the entry into the Promised Land through the Exile into Babylon, scriptures were most often relayed to the listener by one who memorized the text and stories. When the Exiles returned from Babylon two major events took place: (1) the creation of a place where people could worship and learn in their local areas (the synagogue system) and (2) the deliberate process of writing down the stories of the Jewish people. In the Synagogue, scripture reading was of utmost importance. A reading from the Law, the Torah, was presented to the people for their hearing and for them to discuss. Jesus was heard reading the scripture in the Synagogue of his home town. *When he came to Nazareth, where he had been brought up, he went to the synagogue on the sabbath day, as was his custom. He stood up to read, and the scroll of the prophet Isaiah was given to him.* (Luke 4:16-17a)

Before the Gospels were written (the earliest was the Gospel of Mark which dates 60-65), those in the new community, often called The Way, gathered to tell the stories of Jesus by those who had been eye-witnesses or stories told by those who heard the story from an eye-witness.

In the traditional/classical form of worship (often called "liturgical"), scripture continues to play a central role. Most often there are, at minimum, two scripture texts read during a worship service. Traditionally, the readings include a reading from the Old Testament, a reading from a Psalm, a reading from the Letters or Epistles and concludes with a reading from the Gospel (which typically is the focus text of the day). There is a special feeling which floats across the soul when, at the end of a reading, the liturgist or pastor declares, "The Word of God for the People of God" and in response comes the echo, "Thanks be to God."

Wesleyan:

John Wesley wrote in his *Preface to Sermons: "I want to know one thing,—the way to heaven; ... He hath written it down in a book. O give me that book! At any price, give me the book of God! I have it: here is knowledge enough for me. Let me be homo unius libri."* *(A man of one book)* This "book" was so important that in Wesley's instructions to the new church in the Americas he listed in his Sunday Service the specific instructions: a chapter from the Old Testament and a chapter from the Gospels. These are accompanied by readings from the Psalms and Epistles. For Wesley, one is to be a person of the "book" and one can only be that if one abides in that "book." Worship was bathed in the words of scripture for in scripture one found the way to God.

Practical Theology For Today:

Over the years I have experienced a decrease in the amount of scripture used in worship. Too often these readings are deleted so the preacher has more time to preach. (I will address more on this topic in the "Sermon" section.)

In a conversation Dr. Leonard Sweet, my Doctor of Ministry mentor at United Theological Seminary, he told me of his realization that he had "a bad case of verse-itis." Dr. Sweet defined the word by saying he knew a lot of "verses" from the Bible but not many "stories" from the Bible. Even Wesley understood that people in general do not spend time with the Bible and for many the only time they hear scriptures is in the hour of worship.

Too often those who preach insert scripture in a cut-and-paste fashion so they can create some context of authenticity for what they are saying. A verse here and a piece of a verse there are enough. This reflects the concept of an old hair product which proclaimed "Just a little dab will do ya!"

I have also become aware of the varied translations now used in worship. What concerns me most are those who read from paraphrased Bibles or text that are not accepted as accurate translations. I sense many will use the translation that says what they want it to say or that sounds more contemporary. Paraphrases and blended texts of paraphrase and translation are great for devotional settings. However, when it comes to the place of reading a text in worship I want it to be from the most accurate translation available so what the listener hears is the Word of God and not the "word" I want them to hear.

If we as ministers are called to be the "proclaimers of the Word," it is our responsibility and obligation to be sure those under our care hear the Word.

CREED/AFFIRMATION OF FAITH

Worship Tradition:

After the church was set free to worship and exist without fear by Constantine's Edict of Milan, which legalized Christianity over the Roman Empire, the "church" which was both underground and isolated rose to the surface. Once in the sunlight they quickly discovered there were differing opinions within the context of their polity (organization) and theology. Most prominent among those issues concerned the divinity of Jesus. As they began quarreling with each other about what the core doctrines of the faith should be, Emperor Constantine called a synod of the church leaders, using a vernacular term, to get their act together. Constantine sent notices of invitation to 1800 Bishops of the church. Those attending numbered between 250 and 318 depending on which list you read. The Nicene Council convened in 325 A.D. Two very important items on the agenda were establishing a date for Easter and the resolving issues concerning the divinity of Christ.

A group called Arians said Jesus was not an eternal part of the Father but came into being at a very specific time and was subservient to the Father. Other Gnostic groups said Jesus was not human and was only an illusion. They declared that Jesus did not really die on the cross, and some went so far as to say it was an avatar of Jesus, not Jesus himself, on the cross. The Council denounced those concepts and accepted as doctrine the understanding Jesus was *homoousious*, or of the same

Substance and Spirit of God, and was indeed in the beginning with God.

The end result was twofold. First, it was recognized there were indeed differences between the churches in "polity" (how they conduct their business and even structure their worship) which should be recognized. Second, there are core Christian doctrines which, if individuals call themselves Christian, must accept as unchangeable. Thus they created the *Nicene Creed*, a "credo" statement that declares "This I Believe." Each section of the Creed defines what the Church had determined as unquestionable.

First the definition of God:

We believe in one God, the Father Almighty, the maker of heaven and earth, of things visible and invisible.

Second, a very detailed description of who Jesus is combating the heresies of the day:

And in one Lord Jesus Christ, the Son of God, the begotten of God the Father, the Only-begotten, that is of the essence of the Father. God of God, Light of Light, true

God of true God, begotten and not made; of the very same nature of the Father,

by Whom all things came into being, in heaven and on earth, visible and invisible.

Who for us humanity and for our salvation came down from heaven, was incarnate, was made human, was born perfectly of the holy virgin Mary by the Holy Spirit. By whom He took body, soul, and mind, and everything that is in man, truly and not in semblance. He suffered, was crucified, was buried, rose again on the third day, ascended into heaven with the same body, [and] sat at the right hand of the Father. He is to come with the same body and with the glory of the Father, to judge the living and the dead; of His kingdom there is no end.

Third, the image of the Holy Spirit:

We believe in the Holy Spirit, in the uncreated and the perfect; Who spoke through the Law, prophets, and Gospels; Who came down upon the Jordan, preached through the apostles, and lived in the saints.

Finally, standard doctrines:

We believe also in only One, Universal, Apostolic, and [Holy] Church;

in one baptism in repentance, for the remission, and forgiveness of sins;

and in the resurrection of the dead,

in the everlasting judgment of souls and bodies,

and the Kingdom of Heaven and in the everlasting life.

In a practical understanding, the Creed was designed to put a fence around our faith in order to keep out heresy and to create for us a bedrock foundation of what we who call ourselves Christian believe.

Wesleyan:

When Wesley sent the Americans the *Sunday Service* he placed in the liturgy not the Nicene but the

Apostle's Creed. The purpose is to give those gathered an opportunity to declare what they believe. The creed outlines our theology. When the community stands and "declares" their faith it is not intended to be a meek and humble event but a bold affirmation. The Apostle's Creed is simpler and also more rhythmic so the congregation finds it easier to declare in a choral response.

First, the creed defines God the Father:
> *I believe in God, the Father Almighty,*
> *maker of heaven and earth;*

Second, the creed defines for us who Jesus is:
> *And in Jesus Christ his only Son, our Lord;*
> *who was conceived by the Holy Spirit,*
> *born of the Virgin Mary,*
> *suffered under Pontius Pilate,*
> *was crucified, dead, and buried;*
> *He descended into hell (or to the dead)*
> *the third day he rose from the dead;*
> *he ascended into heaven,*
> *and sitteth at the right hand of*
> *God the Father Almighty;*
> *from thence he shall come to*
> *judge the quick and the dead.*

Thirdly, the creed identifies the Third Person of the Trinity as well as the broader aspects of the faith:

> *I believe in the Holy Spirit, the holy catholic church, the communion of saints the forgiveness of sins, the resurrection of the body, and the life everlasting. Amen.*

We may not agree on the exact order of worship. We do not all agree on the music we sing. We may not even agree on what the preacher/pastor should wear on Sunday morning. But the Creed declares in spite of all our differences and opinions, these are beliefs that allow us to call ourselves Christian. To believe otherwise is heresy.

The inclusion in Wesley's Sunday Service implicates the importance and centrality of the Creed as well as the Lord's Prayer.

Practical Theology For Today:

To arbitrarily leave the elements of the Lord's Prayer and the Creed out of worship is, in a very true sense, non-Wesleyan. Yet it is quite evident these two foundational elements of worship are the first to disappear when structuring a contemporary/post-modern worship service (and sometimes in the traditional/classical worship) – primarily to make room for more music and a longer sermon.

For some it is a statement which seems foreign and antiquated - *sitteth at the right hand ... from thence he shall come to judge the quick and the dead?* Beyond those Shakespearian phrases two in particular cause concern: *He descended into hell (or descended to the dead)* and *the holy catholic church.*

The phrase *He descended into hell (or descended to the dead)* mysteriously disappeared from the Creed shortly after Wesley send over the Sunday Service.

During my time at Emory University there were scholars searching for a date or reason for the loss but, at my last hearing, no definitive explanation had been agreed upon. Some reported the "Protestants" wanted to delete the phrase because it seemed – well – too "Catholic" saying it referred to purgatory.

The reason for the statement comes from the struggle at the Nicene Council. The early church struggled against many false doctrines. Some said Jesus was simply a good man called by God to do a mission. Others said he was more of an angel and simply appeared one day and began a ministry. The statement directly addresses the false doctrine declaring Jesus did not really die on the cross but was somehow mysteriously transported to Heaven before he died. This statement was included in the creed to offer an understanding that Jesus really did die. The Nicene Creed addresses this concern by stating *was buried.* To clarify the misunderstanding, in the Apostle's Creed it was not about purgatory but to make the bold statement Jesus *descended into hell (or descended to the dead)* meant Jesus REALLY DIED on the cross – and then came back to life on Easter morn. It was placed to add emphasis: *was crucified,* ***dead****, and* ***buried****.* When the statement is proclaimed by the believer that person acknowledges Jesus' true suffering and real death. The statement concludes with the recovery – *and rose from the dead.*

The other troubling statement is *I believe in… the holy catholic church.* The issue with those uninformed is the association with "holy catholic church" with the Roman Catholic Church. Perpetuation of that understanding can be stopped by simply educating the congregation on what they are saying. The word is "catholic" with a small "c." If one reads the history of the church he or she would discover the church was singular until 1054 A.D. when the Roman Church and the Eastern Church divided. Both are "Catholic" with a capital "C." Martin Luther created the first major shift away from Catholic. But the little "c" was there in the creed before there were divisions.

So often we put an asterisk "*" next to the word "catholic" and footnote a definition that the word means "universal." Some congregations go so far as to insert the word "universal" into the creed. In response to that change I have two statements. First, to me there is a difference between "catholic" and "universal." In my finite mind "universal" establishes a specific space or boundary. The word "catholic" is larger than universal. It stretches both to the highest heights and the widest widths of all creation. It is boundless.

The second response is theological and literary. If someone decides simply to change a word in the Creed what keeps others from also changing words in the Lord's Prayer, or Psalm 23, or even passages of scripture that causes them distress and discomfort?

By its very nature "Credo" is a bold statement of belief. It is not something which should be blandly mumbled or gently whispered. The Creed is a declaration – one which should inspire a believer to powerfully proclaim "This I Believe!"

SERMON

Worship Tradition:

To proclaim the word of the Lord is nothing new. The primary task of the prophet was to declare to the people "Thus says the Lord!" More often than not the declaration focused on the waywardness of the people and the call to return to a Godly Standard. As biblical history tells us, even though the "word" was bold the reception by the Children of Israel was cool. During the time of the unified and divided kingdoms the prophets were the preachers. When a person went to the Temple he/she might hear the priest lead worship and offer prayers, but it was the voice of the prophet that carried a tone of authority.

After the Babylonian Exile and the Synagogue system was established, the order of service called for the leader to offer a commentary on the scriptures read. Once when Jesus returned to his hometown Nazareth he joined in the worship experience. He read the text for the day and then offered a commentary. True to prophetic form, Jesus was then run out of town. Jesus himself, in the Sermon on the Mount and in several instances of debate, sounds like a preacher.

The sermon was a natural flow into the new community called Christians. It began in Acts with Peter's preaching and Paul followed suit. It was a conduit for spreading the Word. Romans chapter 10 illustrates the need for proclamation: *But how are they to call on one in whom they have not believed? And how are they to believe in one of whom they have never heard? And how are they to hear without someone to proclaim him?* (Romans 10:14 NRSV)

I must say, for almost 1500 years the sermon was <u>not</u> the main focal point of worship. Worship centered on the celebration of the Lord's Supper. The sermon was, in a true sense, a homily – a commentary on the scriptures of the day. (The modern-day definition of homily is a short sermon.)   The unified church divided in 1054 but remained central in its effort by working cooperatively. The sound of a crashing hammer in 1517 when Martin Luther nailed his thesis on the church door led to the establishment of a Church in Protest (better understood as the Protestant Movement) and began the true move away from the unified body of Christ. Luther created a worship experience with emphasis on music and preaching and the Eucharistic moment was simply another function of the liturgy. It was Luther who moved the sermon to a new role as the center/primary function in worship.

I will not go into great detail here regarding the historic impact of preaching on the Protestant Church. I do go into great detail in a previous work titled *Gospeltelling to a Digital Culture: The Forensic Reconstruction of a Good Story* (Wyndham Hall Press, 2007). There I trace the growth and expansion of the Protestant Church through its powerful preachers and proclaimers of the Word.

Wesleyan:

In the *Sunday Service* Wesley inserts the sermon after the Creed. There is no direction as to outline or pattern or even length. For the most part John Wesley wrote his sermons out in full and read them from the pulpit. Charles Wesley, on the other hand, found freedom in extemporaneous preaching. The one primary lesson to be learned from John Wesley regarding preaching is simply be prepared. Preaching is serious business. To enter the pulpit with a text and the hope the Spirit will move and direct is not a part of his homiletical understanding. There is no scriptural text saying that those called to "preach" will never have to study and prepare because God will give then all the words they need to say right after the reading of the morning text.

Practical Theology For Today:

The sermon is very personal. Sermons reflect the character, doctrine, and belief system of the one called to proclaim the Word. The old adage of creating a sermon containing an introduction, three points, and a poem has long since disappeared. In fact, the understanding of expository preaching, the developing a sermon around a text of scripture, has almost vanished.

Today, in both the contemporary/post-modern and in the traditional/classical form of worship the sermon has moved from being scripture based to theme based. In times past the lectionary pattern provided a deliberate model for preaching the life and teachings of Christ. Now there is more emphasis on what I term "self-help" messages. How to have a better marriage. How to raise a family. How to love your spouse. How to be financially stable. In these sermons, and I speak from one who now listens to others preach, you could remove a couple of statements and they would fit into any positive thinking seminar. As a people who once prided themselves on being people of the Book we no longer teach and preach the Book. It appears the church desires sermons in series rather than sermons on Biblical texts. (Then I wonder, is it the choice of the people or the intention of the preacher?)

When I have conducted seminars on preaching, I ask those preachers this question: "When you examine your collection of sermons, are you preaching more from Paul than you are from the Gospels?" I have all my sermons saved electronically but I also have a hard-copy file where I not only save the sermon but also the notes from my research on that sermon. I have these hard-copies in a five-drawer file cabinet. The first three drawers are sermons from the Gospels. There may be half a drawer on sermons preached from the Letters and Epistles. And the remaining space is filled with Old Testament text sermons. My call is to preach Christ and if Paul fits in somewhere I will throw him in once in a while. Paul is good but Jesus is Savior. I will take his work over everyone else.

I am personally bothered by ministers who reserve forty-five minutes for their sermons. They often wonder why people do not feel a sense of "connection to God" or "presence of the Spirit." The reason is there is no room. I sense they are more concerned about hearing their own voices than giving the congregation a chance to hear the voice of God. They reduce the "up front" worship experience by leaving out a song or two, forget the Creed and Lord's Prayer, and then they may read a single verse or brief passage. If worshipers are lucky, they may hear that verse repeated in the sermon.

In what is often called the Primitive Church, the stories of Jesus and the gathering around the Table of Remembrance were the focal points of worship. The "sermon" was a simple expository word reflecting of the Word. Now the worship experience has shifted and the "Word" has been reduced and almost negated in order that the preacher can get to his/her "word." In doing so the focus is redirected from "how great God is" to "how great I can preach."

OCCASIONAL ELEMENTS

The last two units are vital elements but are not a part of a weekly worship service in most United Methodist churches. Those two elements are Communion and Baptism. I am not breaking these into the historical connections but rather will simply address their uniqueness within our Methodist tradition.

COMMUNION/LORD'S SUPPER/EUCHARIST

We gather around the table to receive the gifts of bread and wine for one reason – Jesus told us to do it. Jesus instructs in Luke 22:19: *"Do this in remembrance of me."*

Wesley, in his Anglican way, admonishes us to hear the instruction of the Church: *"The Church gives a particular direction with regard to those that are in Holy Orders: 'In all cathedral and collegiate Churches and Colleges, where there are many Priests and Deacons, they shall all receive the communion with the Priest, every Sunday at the least.'" (The Duty of Constant Communion* By John Wesley, Sermon 101, 1872.) This weekly desire seemed to have had a short life in the "frontier" church of the Americas as clergy were stretched thin and churches did not have clergy present every Sunday.

It seems to have become our tradition to offer the sacrament monthly and on special occasions such as Ash Wednesday, Holy Thursday, and Christmas Eve. If I may voice a pet-peeve, it bothers me when the minister leads in the liturgy and stumbles over the words or when it seems to be "work" just to finish the text. Ministers do this on a regular basis! Most could recite the text if they would simply let go of the book. This is a holy moment. This is a sacred event. If the clergy do not prepare themselves spiritually and textually for the sanctity of the moment neither will those receiving experience the holiness of the gift.

BAPTISM

If there is any singular theology in the church where more battles take place it is in the arena of Baptism. We continue to struggle with clergy who ignore the mandate of the Discipline and "rebaptize" persons. We debate with the laity who see no problem with being baptized over and over again. Again, here is a place where persons should be instructed in membership classes as to the theology of the church. We seem to have a hard time making the statement: "If you do not believe or abide by the acts, actions, and Discipline of the United Methodist Church then maybe this is not the church for you." We often anchor ourselves in a delusional place thinking we are the "best" church for everyone. I have often said that in God's great wisdom there has been a church established for each and every one of us. Simply stated, whatever you believe, however you want to worship, whichever peer group you wish to associate with there is a church for you. And if I may be so bold, don't try to change my church for it is because of its theology and polity I am proud of my membership and ordination.

In regards to the act of baptism itself, we are not given specific instructions in Biblical text as to "how" to baptize. Some hold to the theory that the only way to baptize is by immersion. This raises the question: "Was Jesus baptized by immersion?" In Mark's Gospel it reads: *And just as he was coming up out of the water ....* (Mark 1:10). But what does "coming up out of the water" mean? Does it mean Jesus was being lifted up from underneath the water or does it mean as he was coming up (walking) out of the River Jordan?

Wesleyan/Methodist take a broad approach to the "how" of baptism and I have conducted this sacrament in all three ways, immersion, pouring, and sprinkling, to persons of all ages. The mandate is that a person is baptized only one time.

I offer again the same challenge for the act of baptism as I did in the offering up of communion – when you do it, do it well and do it once.

CONCLUSION

The traditional / classical worship should embrace each of these attributes of worship simply because that is what "traditional/classical" worship focuses upon.

For those in the contemporary / post-modern style of worship, who claim the name of Methodist/Wesleyan, I see no reason for those to cast out all the elements of historical worship simply because they consider it "old school." There are some elements of worship by which we are identified as Wesleyan / Methodist such as the Lord's Prayer, Creed, the sanctity of Communion, and the boldness of our singing.

Much of the struggle over the structure of worship occurs when churches place persons, many times from other liturgical traditions or lack thereof, in positions of worship leadership with no background in Wesleyan tradition. They do not have a vested interest in retaining parts of the worship order that they deem unnecessary or confusing. It is precisely at this point the Church should mandate itself to do a better job of preparing the laity for service in the Wesleyan/Methodist tradition.

Pat Summitt, past head basketball coach for the University of Tennessee, has been diagnosed with Alzheimer's disease. In a recent interview I heard her describe the tragic loss of memories. She described it this way: "Have you ever walked along an ocean shoreline, only to look back and realize your footprints have washed away? That's what Alzheimer's is like." This is my greatest fear for the people called United Methodist – we forget who we are - when those in the Wesleyan tradition look back and see no footsteps of those who brought us this far.

More and more I experience the moving away from tradition in the United Methodist Church. We have indeed bowed to the idol of being all things to all people and pay homage to the notion that we must abandon any evidence of being tied to a denomination in order to attract persons into our churches. The words of Bishop Canon have indeed come full circle. In our effort to be "all things to all people" in many places we have become something other than Methodist.

About The Author

Jonathan Watts is the Director of Religious Studies at Snead State Community College and the John Wesley Professor of Homiletics and Biblical Studies for the Graduate Theological Foundation. He educational background includes a Master of Divinity from Candler School of Theology, Emory University; a Doctor of Ministry from United Theological Seminary, and a Ph.D. from The Graduate Theological Foundation doing work in the United States and at Oxford University, Oxford England. Dr. Watts defended his dissertation at Christ Church College, Oxford University. In 2011 he was awarded the title of Oxford Foundation Fellow after doing research after doing research at Oxford University.

Dr. Watts has published two books: Gospeltelling to a Digital Culture: The Forensic Reconstruction of a Good Story and The Battle Lines of Worship: Finding a Place of Truce and Trust (both available through Wyndham Hall Press).